It's Okay Not to Be Fabulous Every Day!

by

Ally Dalsimer

IT'S OKAY NOT TO BE FABULOUS EVERY DAY!

This eBook is licensed for your personal enjoyment only. This eBook may not be re-sold or given away to other people. If you're reading this eBook and did not purchase it, or it was not purchased for your use only, please return it and purchase your own copy. Thank you for respecting the hard work of the author.

Copyright © 2023 ALLY DALSIMER. All rights reserved, including the right to reproduce this book, or portions thereof, in any form. No part of this text may be reproduced, transmitted, downloaded, decompiled, reverse engineered, or stored in or introduced into any information storage and retrieval system, in any form or by any means, whether electronic or mechanical without the express written permission of the author. The scanning, uploading, and distribution of this book via the Internet or via any other means without the permission of the author and publisher is illegal and punishable by law. Please purchase only authorized electronic editions and do not participate in or encourage electronic piracy of copyrighted materials. Thank you.

The publisher does not have any control over and does not assume any responsibility for author or third-party websites or their content.

Cover designed by Telemachus Press, LLC

Cover art created by Lea Waldridge

Interior art:
Copyright© iStock/1367839752/SpicyTruffel

Publishing services by Telemachus Press, LLC
7652 Sawmill Road
Suite 304
Dublin, Ohio 43016
http://www.telemachuspress.com

Visit the author on:
  Twitter: @DalsimerAlly
  Facebook: Ally Dalsimer – Author
  Instagram: Ally.Dalsimer
  Website: AllyDalsimer.com
  LinkedIn: Ally Dalsimer

ISBN: 978-1-956867-60-2 (eBook)
ISBN: 978-1-956867-61-9 (Paperback)
ISBN: 978-1-956867-62-6 (Hardcover)

Library of Congress Control Number: 2023902742

Version 2023.03.13

What people are saying about,
It's Okay Not to Be Fabulous Every Day!

"Through stories and anecdotes, we see how powerful it is to not only have dreams but to survive the harsh disruptions of hate and havoc. In '*Fabulous,*' Ally Dalsimer skillfully walks us through her journey out of depression and into a self-reliant, self-fulfilling life."

–Hope Clark, Executive Director, United Way Kent County, MD; Founder, Wheelbarrow Productions, Inc.

"Who among us hasn't felt defeated, depressed, anxious and generally overwhelmed by "this weird journey we call life"? Luckily for us, Ally shares with the reader some common human experiences, offering helpful suggestions on how to get through these difficult times. I read the book and got inspired by it!"

–Kathy Kinzer, Education Support Specialist, Northern Virginia Community College

"Ally Dalsimer has written something that is relatable, real and needs to be shared with the world. *Fabulous* gives us insights into a side of leadership we don't see very often—the raw, real passion that one needs to live a genuine life and go beyond just dreaming."

–Brandon Russell, Political Strategist, CEO of Russell & Team Inc.

If you have a few minutes, please consider leaving an honest online review. It can be brief—as little as a sentence or two. By sharing if you liked this book or not and why, you help other readers decide if *It's Okay Not to Be Fabulous Every Day!* is right for them.

I read all comments, so look forward to hearing from you.

It's Okay Not to Be
Fabulous
Every Day!

How it all began

I BEGAN THIS compilation late summer 2019 with the intent of providing a bit of life-guidance for my kids to use as they launched into the world. The original title was Electric Blue Typewriter, and my introductory page read:

Advice from life's encounters, movies, books, and who knows what else. Here are tips I've gleaned that I'm sharing to help you deal with the ups and downs, ins and outs, and vagaries of this weird journey we call 'life.'

Never forget that all the lessons you need to be "successful" you learned in kindergarten: say please and thank you, share, work hard, play fair, and clean up after yourselves. And if you only do one thing, make it to:

'Live the Golden Rule'

- ✔ *Be kind*
- ✔ *Be good*
- ✔ *Be humble*

Or, alternatively, 'do unto others as you would have others do unto you:'

- ✔ Treat people with respect and kindness (walk away if they don't treat you the same)
- ✔ Talk to others the way you'd like them to talk to you (stop talking to them if they are rude or abrasive)
- ✔ Listen when other people speak (rather than think about the point you want to make next)
- ✔ Help when and as you are able (but don't harm yourself in the process)

I love you both!!

Then life got busy: house flood, a run for Congress, caring for my aging mother (while still campaigning), my mom's death, and finally getting the kids off to school. The Electric Blue Typewriter got put on a shelf and forgotten. Until now.

Is this book for you?

THIS BOOK IS a compilation of sayings, quotes, observations, and other nuggets of wisdom and interest gleaned from a wide array of sources that help me confront and conquer adversities on a daily basis. I share them here in hopes they help you too.

> *"This book is for people of all shapes, sizes, colors, and backgrounds."*

If you want a comprehensive self-help book that provides instruction on how to achieve long-term career or life goals in six easy steps, or maximize your potential based on a stepwise pyramid, or save the world by engaging in five key activities, or get rich by investing in unexpected ways, or find your personal god through guided meditation, or whatever, then this book is not for you.

This book is for people of all shapes, sizes, colors, and backgrounds who are busy or not busy, working or not working, old or young, gender conforming or not who would like some help finding kindness and self-love as they circumnavigate the pebbles and boulders that trip us up as we make our way along the path of life's journey. In short, it's for anyone who wants a brief talisman to staying sane in crazy times.

So, if you want to deal with daily struggles without becoming a basket case, to handle adversity and rejection with positivity, to keep moving forward without becoming despondent, to live with purpose without self-sabotage or recrimination, or simply to find a way to be the best person you personally can be, then please read on. This book is for you!

Enjoy, and be well!

Ally Dalsimer

Grief is the price we pay for love
—Queen Elizabeth, II

I RECENTLY GOOGLED how to achieve 'life goals.' There are lots of books and websites out there, offering in detail what and how to live based on specific steps or categories. Over the years, I've tried following various steps, developing habits, and embracing methods. And while I've learned a lot from my readings and research, and have achieved a great deal, there are still moments, days, weeks when I feel like a complete failure.

That's when the self-recrimination kicks in—I can't even succeed when given instructions! 'Failing' left me anxious and unhappy, and wondering what is so wrong with me that I flopped at what others seem to do with ease.

Ah, but that's just it: a lot of people are this way!

People everywhere are dealing with multiple stressors: economic uncertainties, social and political inequities, global warming and associated natural disasters, rising crime rates, COVID, famine, war, and on and on. In this time of personal and global insecurity, it's natural for us to search for answers, which is probably why there is an upsurge in articles, books, and social media posts on self-care, on manifesting, on taking charge of our destinies.

> *"It's natural for us to
> search for answers."*

I am no different. My life has been turbulent and unpredictable. Over the last few years, I've dealt with my husband's death, my mother's death, three house floods, children struggling with mental health and physical injuries, job loss, start and failure of a new business, running for public office, and now launching into an entirely new field.

My journey may be different from yours, but only in its details.

Back to a couple months ago, as I woke one gloomy morning to the harsh realities that the kids were gone and needing me much less, my business was floundering, I still hadn't finished unpacking about a dozen of the boxes left over from the last house flood and, no matter many times I went over to sort through her belongings, my mom's apartment remained as she'd left it when she died. What a slouch I was, unable to accomplish tasks that everyone else seems to manage! I'll do better tomorrow, yes tomorrow.

But, when morning came, nothing changed.

The idea of unpacking those boxes, cleaning out the closets, sorting through the museum that was once my mom's apartment seemed too much. The edges of a dark sadness flittered into consciousness, threatening to roll over me, into me.

And then I remembered the Electric Blue Typewriter folder.

I read every scrap of paper in the folder and felt better. Funny how we often forget to take our own advice. With an adjusted attitude, I determined to reframe what 'success' meant for me, and gave myself 2 years to figure out what to do with my life.

A journey of 1,000 miles begins with a single step

—Lao Tzu

USUALLY, I'M UP by 6 a.m. This morning, I finally pushed myself to a vertical position somewhere around 10. Having gone to bed before 9 the night before, you'd think I'd have been well-rested. Instead, it felt like walking through molasses making my way to the kitchen to feed my hungry cat.

I glanced at the long 'to do' list and pile of papers waiting patiently on my desk—they judged me, chided me. The solid gray sky was leaking a constant drizzle of chilly wet tentacles worming their way into my bones, though I was warm and dry behind the window.

After a concerted effort to muster the energy to do more than look at the stack of papers, I remembered my resolution to reframe 'success' and be my own best cheerleader; I moved the bar for today's accomplishments.

Instead of turning on my computer and working my way through the list and pile, I pointed my slippered feet back towards the bedroom and, by midday, I'd stripped the bed, done a load of laundry, made soup and played with the cat. That seemed like enough. So, I curled up under a blanket and watched movies until it was time to brush teeth and get back in bed.

> *"The truth is some days it's harder to be 'all that' than others."*

Instead of feeling depressed or berating myself for not working my way through the day's lengthy list, I'd set new milestones and conquered them. Congratulations to me! I had homemade soup to eat and clean sheets to sleep in, my cat was content, and I saw a couple great flicks. All good.

The truth is some days it's harder to be 'all that' than others, and it's not only okay but vital that we shift, morph, and flex to better embody the proverbial tree bending with the wind so it doesn't break.

Just keep swimming, just keep swimming
—Dory, *Finding Nemo*

IT SEEMS TO be working!

The days of self-flagellation for failing to 'accomplish' substantive tasks are gone. I'm tired of society dictating what success is for me, judging me against an arbitrary standard and, worse, feeling bad when I fail to meet that standard.

"To live is to face adversity."

To live is to face adversity, whether continual or episodic. Sometimes we must push through and sometimes we conquer gloriously. What none of us wants is to get sucked into a downward spiral leading to mental or physical collapse … it's just too hard to put ourselves back together. Regardless of the challenge, what matters is not giving up and not giving in.

Forward focus through present action.

There is a saying that it's not our struggles that define our character, it's how we deal with those struggles that defines us. These last few years have been truly challenging for me. Focusing on the glass half full and finding ways to stay positive while dealing with negative circumstances keeps me sane. That doesn't mean being a complete Pollyanna; it means being kind to oneself, embracing patience and forgiveness.

> *"It's a whole lot easier to float than to recover from drowning."*

It doesn't matter if we're not moving much at any one point in time. What matters is continuing our journey, recognizing that how (and how fast) we keep swimming will be different for each of us. What matters is to keep on keepin' on, even if we have to take an occasional break, because it's a whole lot easier to float for a time than it is to recover from drowning.

I confess that I have been as blind as a mole, but it is better to learn wisdom late than never to learn it at all

—Sherlock Holmes

FRIENDS HAVE REMARKED that I am a 'very strong' person. Maybe that's true; maybe not. I was raised to be self-sufficient, not to ask for help or show weakness. I worked hard to appear strong, to seem happy, to not give in to depression or numbing paralysis, at least not publicly. But is that really strength?

Allowing oneself to grieve, to wallow, to explore the darker side of the emotional spectrum provides a yin to life's yang. It's okay to feel sad, to need alone time, to cry, and to ask for help when you need it.

All of us must deal with hardship and strife of one flavor or another. While unique, hardships share one commonality: they are often out of our control. We can't control, for example, if a loved one dies of cancer or if a storm destroys our home or if we lose our job due to cutbacks.

All we truly control is what we do, how we react, and how we choose to go forward.

Emerson wrote about life being a journey, not a destination, and we've all been admonished to 'stop and smell the roses.' The more our technology advances, the faster-paced our lives become and the less we listen to the wisdom of those who preceded us.

Philosophers like Socrates, Aristotle, and Plato spent hours each day exploring the majestic landscapes of their inner thoughts. Today, we have more knowledge yet understand a great deal less than they did. Taking time to slow our bodies and quiet our minds liberates and empowers us.

We have all the tools we need within us to maximize our personal potentials.

Visualizing our end point will help us realize it. Once we know what the goal is, we can create a mental blueprint for how to get there, identifying the incremental steps we need to take. Along the way, we will find the strength and courage we need by seeking out those who are helpful and kind, rebuffing and avoiding those who are not, and congratulating ourselves for all accomplishments, no matter how small.

The words you speak become the house you live in

—Hafiz

IT'S A UNIVERSAL truth that if we don't keep moving forward, we'll be swallowed by the past, stagnating in a never-ending Groundhog Day loop that inevitably leaves us empty and unfulfilled.

> "Taking action, any action, is a feat unto itself."

To experience inner joy and self-worth, to value ourselves and find meaning in our existence, we must bravely face the unknown and advance into it. We must decide to act and keep doing so day after day. It doesn't matter if the action is small or large—both are accomplishments.

The hard part? Getting started.

Getting started is half the battle. Taking action, any action, is a feat unto itself and should be encouraged and rewarded. Regardless of the task, if we make a start, we are halfway to finishing! Super over-achievers aside, we mere mortals struggle with routinely embracing fabulousness.

Seriously, who can be fabulous every single day? Not me.

The key is not to get discouraged when we have 'one of those days (or weeks).' It's okay if our paths are not linear—taking small steps or a few side steps is better than sliding backwards.

What matters is that, if we truly want to live our dream, it's up to us to make it happen. Let's encourage and reward ourselves for what we do, rather than berate ourselves for what we don't do.

If we are kind to ourselves along the journey, we will get there faster and with less unhappiness.

Do, or do not. There is no try

—Yoda

WHEN WE'RE YOUNG, we all dream about what we'll grow up to be and do, yet 95% of us never attain our dreams or our life's desire. Why? Maybe we didn't set specific, realistic, and achievable milestones; maybe it's because we don't face the future consistently and with determination.

Succeeding in our chosen endeavor takes effort. Everything we do takes effort. Reminding ourselves it's okay if our paths aren't linear, that we are free to shift directions as our life goals change, gives us the freedom to do the work in harmony with life's ebbs and flows.

If it's important, we'll do it. Or will we?

Easy example: lots of us say we want to lose weight. Definitely doable. Or is it? If we don't identify specific behavioral changes to implement, the goal is too amorphous. It's not rocket science: give up processed foods and refined sugars, exercise daily, track and record weekly progress. Boom. The hitch? How many of us are willing to make those changes? Is the long-term objective of losing say 20 pounds worth skipping that second slice of pizza or a caramel macchiato now?

For most of us, no. And that's when we find ourselves in an endless feedback loop of self-recrimination continually deceiving ourselves that 'cheating' today means our ambition is unattainable. Here's the trick: instead of giving up when temporarily stalled, tolerate a moment's rest and embrace the day's potential.

"If we want it, we will find a way."

Changing up our activities frees our brains so we can refocus later.

Same for completing a paper or presentation for work by a specified deadline. There are going to be days when nothing comes together. Instead of sitting at a computer staring at the blinking curser, listen to music or take a walk or play with your dog or call a friend or whatever. Frustrating as we may find any given point in time, that circumstance is a small and temporary obstacle blocking our view to the target.

If we want it, we will find a way.

> *Genius is one percent inspiration and ninety-nine percent perspiration*
>
> — Thomas Edison

IT'S FUNNY HOW what we want to do least is, ironically, what helps us most. For example, when we're sad, all we want is to be alone, closeting ourselves in comfy clothes eating sweet or salty snacks while binge watching our fave shows. Or maybe that's me. Pushing to vertical, dressing, and going for a walk, especially in the sunshine, releases endorphins and oxygenates the blood, and this nearly always makes me feel better.

It's the getting out the door that's the hard part.

For others, socializing in person, on FaceTime, or on the phone is the exact medicine needed to disperse the dark cloud of depression.

My daughter struggled a lot with depression during the lock-down. Aside from a few emails and texts, she lost touch with schoolmates and closeted herself in her room watching 90s sitcom reruns. After weeks of solitude, she finally agreed to reach out to her closest friends.

FaceTiming with them, some of whom she hadn't spoken to in months, turned her world around. She returned to the socially active, effervescent daughter I'd been missing.

> *"If we're in a rut, changing pace can be the kick in the pants we need."*

If we're in a rut, changing pace and pushing ourselves into action can be the kick in the pants we need.

Just do it

—Nike slogan

JUST DO IT is so easy, so simple ... Except for that doing part of the phrase. Personally, I think the journey of a 1,000 miles begins not with taking the first step, but with mustering up the energy, drive, and commitment to take that step.

We must choose to progress through and into our lives if we want to be happy and fulfilled.

And that's not only for lofty life goals like starting a new business or whatever, it's for getting the day-to-day stuff done.

Yesterday, my to do list was:
- ✔ Edit a client document
- ✔ Pay bills
- ✔ Do the laundry
- ✔ Take the trash to the curb
- ✔ Buy stamps
- ✔ Pick up prescription
- ✔ Get the car emissions done and renew my registration

- ✓ Clean out my mom's apartment (this has been on the list since last June)

After feeding the cat and making a hot cup of tea, I began reviewing the client document. My heart wasn't in it. After reading the same paragraph on the second page for the fourth time, it was time to refocus. I did the laundry, got the trash to the curb, and brushed the cat. Paying bills is tough sometimes, and the bad weather disinclined me to do anything that required leaving the house.

You may think it's pathetic or you may think it's amazing, and that's fine. It doesn't matter in the least what anyone thinks but me.

"Let's listen to the universe and shift gears."

It's both easier and harder when you are your own boss. Missing self-appointed deadlines is all too easy, yet also liberating. It's a privilege to have the flexibility to not work on a sad and rainy Friday then to catch up on Saturday when psychic and physical energies align. If we're 'supposed' to complete particular tasks and it's not working out, in as much as we're able, let's listen to the universe and shift gears.

Listening to our inner voice allows us to live a harmonious and peace-filled existence. And that's the key to genuine success. In the end, we are the only ones who control who we are and what we do.

We can always return to the previous task later.

Hard work beats talent when talent doesn't work hard

—Tim Notke

"AH," YOU SAY, "but I have a boss (or teacher) who's given me an assignment." That may be, but the choice to do that task or not is yours and yours alone. If you do it and do it well, you increase the chances of improving your grades or being promoted; if you don't complete the task or do a substandard job, well, you'll be the one experiencing those consequences. Regardless, it's still your choice.

When it comes to our personal goals, both short and long term, who are we cheating if we choose not to work towards them?

- If our intent is to run a 5K with our child two months from now, who does it hurt if we don't ever bother training?
- If we want to lose 10 pounds before a high school reunion, who cares if we sneak ice cream and cookies late at night when no one is looking?

- If we want a promotion at work, who cares if we do shoddy work, skip out on staff meetings, or duck out of the office early?

Ironically, recognizing we are the obstacles standing in the way of achieving our own dreams liberates us to act. When we fail to work towards our own ambitions, we cheat ourselves—no one else suffers if we skip out or take short cuts.

So, do we want to realize our dream or not?

If yes, then we'll do what's needed. If we aren't willing to do what's needed, perhaps a little self-reflection is in order.

All we have to decide is what to do with the time that is given us

—J.R.R. Tolkien, *Lord of the Rings, The Fellowship of the Ring*

Or, said another way ...

One day your life will flash before your eyes. Make sure it's worth watching

—Gerard Way

MY HUSBAND'S AUNT Norma Jean and Uncle Ralph dreamed of going to New Orleans. That was their dream. To go to New Orleans and eat all the wonderful food and listen to music and enjoy themselves for a few days.

To me, this was not a big dream; not unattainable. It wasn't going to space, or playing professional sports, or being on Broadway. It was taking a week off work, booking a room, and either making a 1,000 mile road trip or flying down. They married in their 20s and talked about this trip for decades.

That's not to say they never had fun or led sad lives—the opposite was true. They were active and adventuresome, taking lots of road trips to visit with family along the Eastern seaboard and to watch the leaves turn along the Appalachian trail, but they never made it to New Orleans.

When Ralph died in his late 50s, Norma Jean told me it was her greatest regret that they never went.

Not all goals need to be lofty or grand.

The reason I spent over 30 years working for environmental protections is the same reason I chose to run for public office, and it's the same reason I am now writing this book: to make a positive difference in the world.

This may sound naïve, and perhaps it is. Naïve or not, what drives me, what makes me genuinely happy, is aspiring to be a better person by making the world a better place, even if in a small way.

There's Still Time to Change the Road You're On

—Led Zeppelin

WHEN WE ARE young, we dream and wish and hope, not for material goods, but for meaning-filled lives and lofty intangibles—to be a firefighter (brave and daring), to go to space (exploring and adventuring), to become a nurse or doctor (helping and healing), or to raise amazing kids (nurturing). Too often we put off dreams until they wither from neglect or are overcome by events.

"Too often we put off dreams."

As we age and take on increasing responsibilities, it's easy to get mired in the mundane minutiae of our day-to-day lives. We forget the wonder and excitement we once felt when imagining our futures.

Taking time to self-reflect, to rediscover our passions, helps us redefine what a purpose-filled and successful life is for us.

Our dreams at 30 or 50 or 70 may be the same or may be different from when we were 3, 5, or 7. What's important is rediscovering 'what we want to be when we grow up,' and understanding that we have ability to achieve those dreams.

And I don't mean, 'gosh, I'd love to win the lottery and own a bunch of stuff.' Material goods make our lives easier and definitely provide temporal pleasures, but genuine self-fulfillment comes only from intangibles like having adventures or creating or helping others.

> *"If our dream is genuine, it's not a chore to work towards it."*

It's vital we ask ourselves: What will truly and deeply fulfill us? What will generate authentic happiness with who we are? Once we know that, we can identify and define our path, then take the first of our 1,000 steps. The key is remembering that our path is one of self-discovery, as well as of achievement, and is likely to morph and modify as we ourselves grow and change.

If our dream is genuine, it's not a chore to work towards it.

If we never want to do what's needed to get where we think we want to be, perhaps it's time for some inner reflection. Perhaps what we believe to be our dream is instead one that someone else wants for us, an idea we grew up thinking based on inputs we received rather than outputs we've generated from within.

Pursuing our ambitions by engaging in actions that deliver us ever closer to our dream will bring joy and positivity into our hearts and our lives. Our certainty and confidence will grow with each step we take.

Regret and fear are twin thieves who would rob us of today
—Robert Hastings

So, why do we put off pursuing happiness? Fear.

Only fear can defeat life
—Life of Pi

FEAR OF THE unknown and fear of change are always with us; it's hardwired into our DNA as a once-vital survival mechanism. Whether it's a prodigious change like taking a new job or getting married, or a small one like trying new foods or visiting a new place, taking that first step is challenging. What is new is, by definition, unknown and unfamiliar. And not knowing is scary.

> "The cost of not taking risks may be a lifetime of dissatisfaction."

Yet, fear is an internal obstacle. When we recognize that the obstacles we perceive are based on fears we can overcome, we allow ourselves to find the courage to explore and vanquish future regrets.

When we go boldly into the unknown and fail, our disappointment will be momentary. If we never take the risk, we may end up plagued by a deep and long-lasting sense of remorse, one that gnaws at the edges of our consciousness, lingering until our time is spent.

The cost of not taking risks may be a lifetime of dissatisfaction, of feeling like we've missed out or messed up. In other words, regret.

> *"Preventing defeat is better than trying to cure failure."*

Regret for things we didn't do is always greater and more pervasive than for things we did. Regret for what we wish we'd done can infest our lives, impacting our mental and physical health, overwhelming us in the small hours of the night, making us wonder 'what if' and 'if only.'

While it's hard not to contemplate past mistakes, dwelling on lost opportunities brings only sadness and a risk of getting trapped in an endless loop, dying without manifesting our internal magic by forgetting to live in today.

Preventing defeat is better than trying to cure failure.

*Woman, first denied a soul,
then called mindless, now arisen,
declared herself an entity to be reckoned*

—Suffragette Statue, 1921

WHEN MY GRANDFATHER died in October 1978, my grandmother had never driven a car, didn't know how to write a check, had never worn pants and certainly not shorts, owned no flat shoes, and had never eaten food with her hands (think pizza, hotdogs, etc.). She had little identity outside of her husband and his vocation.

"If you are unhappy, make a change."

When they married, she gave up ice skating, painting, ceramics, and all other activities 'not suitable' for a married woman. My grandfather didn't force or even ask her to stop; it's just what most women did when they got married in the 1920s, and they both accepted this societal norm.

At the same time, there was a small but mighty number of Suffragettes who were unhappy with those societal norms and who worked long and hard to change them. This is how and when the Women's Movement was born.

The lesson: If you are unhappy, make a change.

This applies to all social and political movements, past and present. And it applies to our individual lives as well.

Hatred paralyzes life; love releases it.
Hatred confuses life; love harmonizes it.
Hatred darkens life; love illuminates it

—Dr. Martin Luther King, Jr.

WE INHERENTLY FEAR change, imagining myriad amorphous obstacles and negative consequences, some of which are real but many of which exist only in our minds.

> *"The solution to achieving our potential begins with love."*

It is the insidious nature of fear, based in an all-consuming irrationality, that stepping boldly into the unknown seems like the riskier proposition, but it's not. When we are afraid, we become angry, often lashing out like scared animals. When anger has no basis in fact or reality, it deepens and morphs into hate.

This, then, is where all the negative 'isms' of our world have their start.

The solution to achieving our potential begins with love—first, loving ourselves. Once we truly accept and embrace who we are, it's time to begin our journey towards a fulfilling future.

It doesn't matter if our dream is working towards societal change or traveling the world or raising a large family. What matters is that it's what's right for us, regardless of what anyone else thinks. Understanding we control our behaviors and attitudes frees us to conquer life's obstacles.

We don't control others, but we can influence change.

> *"All we need to triumph is to take the first step."*

People all over the world routinely make a positive difference by leading efforts to inform perceptions resulting in behavioral, societal, and political shifts that make this a better world.

The environmental movement, women's movement, civil rights movement ... all were founded and are sustained by brave and committed believers taking action to influence community, societal, national, and global change.

All we need to triumph is to take the first step and the next and so on.

Win or lose, if we do our level best, we can take pride in our efforts, allowing ourselves to feel a sense of accomplishment for each milestone achieved on the journey towards our dream. That deep sense of satisfaction will fuel the joy within and keep us motivated.

Living a truly joyful life, satisfied with who we are and what we're doing, means preempting a lifetime of 'shoulda, coulda, wouldas' ... if only.

To succeed in life, you need three things:
a wishbone, a backbone, and a funny bone

—Reba McIntyre

AND POSSIBLY A 'to do' list. Whether we strive for societal change or to travel the world or to clean the house, the first step is the most crucial: deciding to do it. Once that's done, it's time to identify the next step and take it.

Our journeys don't have to be linear. Two steps forward, one step back, a step to the side and so on. As long as, over the longer term, we continue to progress, we will expand our self-confidence and internal exultation. That's how to know we are making the right choices.

> "Our journeys don't have to be linear."

Today, I spent a few hours on work-related tasks, took care of some car stuff and ran a few errands, then decided it was too beautiful to stay inside so I took a long walk. In the evening, I played with my cat, exchanged social media posts with my kids, completed a couple crossword puzzles, and went to bed. All in all, a satisfying Saturday.

The trick to ultimately reaching our destinies is to not get derailed by inconsequential tasks or meaningless and dispiriting activities. If we trudge through our days, monotonously repeating meaningless tasks that bring us no joy, then the world is speaking to us.

Let's listen.

Better to be a has-been than a never-was
—Cecil Parkinson

I RAN FOR Congress. I didn't win, but I ran. Better yet, my campaign influenced the incumbent to change his position on several important policies. If I hadn't run, he wouldn't have changed his positions, and I would probably have spent the rest of my days wondering 'what if' ... What if ... What if ... How sad is that?

So, if you have a dream, go for it!

Achieving our dream, no matter what our dream is, is magical and precious and needs nurturing and encouragement.

"If you have a dream, go for it!"

Giving ourselves permission to shift, morph, and flex our activities during tough times, and congratulating ourselves for maintaining an overall course towards whatever makes us happy, means we are succeeding.

What matters is taking advantage of a new day as a fresh start. Getting out of bed is the day's first accomplishment, and then it's on to the next.

Ultimately, all we can do is our best.

If we do our best—and we alone know if we do—we'll dodge the regret bullet. Regardless of the outcome, what matters is making the effort. If we truly give our best effort, we are justified in feeling proud of the outcome regardless of the result.

> *"Ultimately, all we can do is our best."*

For my part, I'm proud that every day I accomplish at least one task. Setting targets, short-term and long-term, then doing what I can to the best of my prevailing wherewithal to realize my goals.

Doing our best is the reward; winning is a bonus.

Making the effort is what counts.

> *It is not our abilities that show what we truly are. It is our choices*

—Albus Dumbledore, Harry Potter and the Chamber of Secrets

WE KNOW INPUTS result in outputs, meaning we will get out what we put in. Garbage in—garbage out. So, if we choose to make the effort, we will be better placed to reap the reward, whatever that reward may be.

- ✓ If we think the government is corrupt, run for office
  - We might affect substantive policy changes.
- ✓ If we are lonely, call or visit with people we know and like.
  - We might feel less alone and fill an afternoon with light and laughter.
- ✓ If we want to save money, stop buying stuff we don't need.
  - We might discover that home-cooked meals taste great and are fun to prepare.

- ✔ If we want our kids to be happy, loving, and well adjusted, then hug them and listen to them and accept them for who they are.
  - We might realize they're the best friends we have.

Achieving our goals takes effort. Whether working to conquer a routine task like doing the laundry so you have clean clothes to wear or more lofty aspirations like owning a business or getting into college, it's a truism that the harder we work, the luckier we'll be.

There are exceptions to this truism, based almost entirely on the negative '-isms' of the world: racism, sexism, anti-whateverism. The inequities plaguing society are varied and pervasive and real. It's a foundational reason I ran for public office: to make a positive difference.

In 20 years, DiMaggio never had to dive for a ball. Funny how that happens

—Lenny Briscoe, *Law and Order*

OUR LIVES ARE comprised of individual moments in time. These moments offer endless opportunities to learn and grow, to change the direction we're heading. What's most important is listening to our inner voice and moving in ways that lead us closer to a soul-deep satisfaction.

Sometimes moving forward means leaving the comfort of the known and moving into new territory (the unknown). But the unknown is scary, you say. To that I say: Just Do It. We all must move forward (progress), or we'll get stuck (stagnate) and end up sad (regret).

Moving out of our comfort zones and being willing to feel unsure or look silly in new situations is critical—this is what a life-well-lived is all about.

The choices we make and actions we take influence our success. If we do what's needed to prepare, we'll be ready when opportunity's window opens.

- Keeping up with homework can help us do better on that pop quiz
- Washing hands properly and frequently can help us avoid the flu that's going around
- Practicing between lessons can help us master the skill better and faster
- Eating healthy and staying hydrated can help us get through the 5-hour traffic jam

Making forward progress over time is what's important, irrespective of how much progress we make in any given day. Sometimes putting off tasks can be beneficial.

"When opportunity knocks, it's up to you to answer it."

We've been told procrastination is a 'productivity killer' and yet it's worth considering how we are defining 'productivity'—it may be that taking a mental break is the best choice for that juncture.

When pursuing our dreams, the work and rest we invest will pay dividends when our chance finally comes. Like my fortune cookie read the other day: When opportunity knocks, it's up to you to answer it.

Luck is what happens when preparation meets opportunity

—Seneca

MY DAUGHTER IS a first-year student at college this year. Yesterday she sent me this series of texts:

> omg
> i got a 98 out of 100 on my math test
> the one I was nervous about but studied really hard for
> i have all A's now!!!

What's amazing about this text is that my daughter had had the flu so missed the pre-test review class and was worried that, if she did poorly, her borderline grade would slip to a B. This was concerning because she wants to transfer to a school requiring a strong GPA for her application to be considered.

"Positive emotions are rewards for taking the right actions."

In our journeys to be the best 'us' we can be, it's important we stay focused on making steady progress towards achieving our dreams, even if our progress is inconsistent. The returns on our investments will manifest a better job, better grades, successful business, stronger family bonds, etc. The trick is to take the next step, to keep swimming, to not be derailed by meaninglessness.

> *"Life hack: remember the Golden Rule."*

Once we start making changes, small or large, we'll know they're right because we'll feel better. Positive emotions are rewards for taking the right actions; for moving in the right direction.

If we are unhappy or angry or anxious, then something is wrong. Negative emotions are a call to action. When we feel them, we need a change, and only we can make that change.

Life hack: remember the Golden Rule.

Time is the most valuable thing a man can spend

—Theophrastus, Greek Philosopher

TODAY IS THE youngest we will ever be; today marks the maximum number of days we have left; today really is the first day of the rest of our lives. It's why we bandy about the 'today is a present' idea.

Accomplishing a long list of tedious tasks may or may not be worthwhile but acting in ways that bring us joy and move us closer to achieving our heart's desire always has value. The expression about life being short so eat more ice cream is, I think, about much more than literally eating ice cream. To me, it means we must embrace the sweetness of life, the people and places that nourish our souls and elevate our moods.

Life is an accumulation of the individual events and people we encounter; each can and should enrich and improve us. If a person, place, or thing brings misery or sadness or turns us into someone we don't like, let's go in a different direction. Let's purge from our lives what makes us miserable.

It might not be easy, but it will be worthwhile.

By minimizing or eliminating the time we spend with negative people and in meaningless situations, we maximize the time and energy we spend engaging in activities and with people who lift and elate us.

The only calibration that counts is how much heart people invest, how much they ignore their fears of being hurt or caught out or humiliated. And the only thing people regret is that they didn't live boldly enough, that they didn't invest enough heart, didn't love enough. Nothing else really counts at all

—Ted Hughes

I READ A study a couple years ago that summarized a survey of the elderly. Following is what they overwhelmingly identified as their biggest regrets, in order of most mentioned. No other answer came close to these four:

- Not asking for help
- Trying to make bad relationships work
- Dwelling on mistakes and shortcomings
- Worrying too much about other people

What all these have in common is that they are all manifestations of fears that led to procrastination which resulted in lost opportunities:

- ✓ Afraid to show weakness or incompetence, so going it alone too long
- ✓ Afraid to admit to ourselves or to others that we made a mistake, or afraid to be on our own again
- ✓ This is actually the definition of regret
- ✓ Afraid of what others think, forgetting what other people think doesn't matter

Whatever our passion—social justice, disaster relief, education—it is up to us to work around obstacles to find new and possibly unorthodox paths leading us to our destinies. What matters is being true to ourselves, being truthful with ourselves, being our true selves, and fighting hard for a future that brings joy, positivity, and satisfaction.

I used to have a sticky note posted in my office that read: *Integrity is doing the right thing. Credibility is consistent integrity.* When we are authentically happy, our joy is infectious, elevating us and spreading light and love to all we encounter.

Mean people suck

—facts

DURING MY CAMPAIGN, one of my opponent's followers began trolling me on Twitter, posting inaccurate information about me and my political positions. I DM'd him asking if he'd like to talk so we could discuss his concerns; he replied with more pretense.

After he 'bombed' an online Meet & Greet (get to know the candidate) by blasting loud music and subjecting our participants to a hardcore graphic pornographic video, I moved on. This was not a person who was interested in dialogue or understanding or doing more than creating havoc and misery.

Here's the truth: believing bringing others down will lift us up is wrong. That's not how the universe works.

When you engage with people who are mean, or oblivious to all but themselves and their needs, or who are always gloomy and never find a silver lining, we allow their hate, solipsism, and pessimism to penetrate and pervade our lives.

Don't let these negative people drag you down into their dark abyss. Release them and move on.

Even if the process is frustrating or scary, it's important to fill our lives with light and positivity, with those who truly want the best for us, and to immerse ourselves in situations that are joyful and lift us up.

People are mean because, at their core, they don't believe in themselves. Whether they are aware of it or not, it is their inner fears and self-loathing that drive them.

Blame is the outgrowth of the need to feel control in one's life

—Toa of Forgiveness, W. Martin

IT'S EASY AND self-comforting to decide external factors are keeping us from achieving our goals and, sometimes, there are factors impeding us. I've definitely been guilty of this, feeling anger and resentment towards other people or circumstances for hindering me in some way. I felt it when my job managing the Natural Resources Program at the Defense Department was eliminated by a Trump Administration political appointee—a 30-year career gone!

And, yet, if not for that, my path may never have veered into the world of political campaigns.

It was my passion for positive political change on climate, healthcare, and education that pushed me into action, that led me to becoming a candidate. Accepting that we cannot control external factors, and understanding that thinking we can control factors outside of ourselves is an illusion, is the first step to taking charge of our destinies.

Rather than fight to swim upstream against immovable objects, we must instead flow like a river over a streambed of pebbles, embracing responsibility for our actions—only our actions. Blaming others for obstacles put in our paths rather than embracing our potential diminishes our horizon and embitters our existence.

If we know what we want and that want is a need, and that need is for an intangible and important objective, we will find a way to get there.

If you've read *The Boys in the Boat*, you'll know what I mean. If you've seen *Rocky*, you'll understand. We are all born with the tools we need to maximize our potential and achieve our dream. Focusing on external factors out of our control are the obstacles we see when we take our eyes off the goal.

If we are still, taking time to reflect, we will hear our inner voices speak to us.

Those voices will guide us, the universe will help us. We cannot control other people or world events; we can only control who we are and what we do. Once we accept that, we will cease to play the blame game, and can focus our energies on maximizing our potential. True happiness comes from within; we can't rely on other people or external circumstance to 'make' us happy.

Poof! You're happy! No, it doesn't work that way.

Advice is a dangerous gift, even from the wise to the wise

—J.R.R. Tolkien

I HAVE A lengthy track record of acting counter to my instincts, making decisions because 'experts' or well-meaning friends or family have told me it's best. Unsurprisingly, I've taken a lot of wrong steps, all because I lacked the confidence (i.e., was afraid) to follow my gut.

> "Sometimes those we are closest to, fail to see what our unique greatness is."

For a variety of reasons, people like making recommendations and do so with remarkable frequency. Much of the time, they barely bother to ask what it is we want, or what our dreams and passions are. Sometimes those we are closest to, the ones we think should be our greatest advocates, fail to see what our unique greatness is. This is especially true if we haven't figured it out for ourselves yet.

If we do know, sharing our deepest dreams and passions is risky because doing so opens us up to criticism and mockery from those we tell. Those we tell may not realize their offhand dismissal or ill-timed chuckle has crushed the burgeoning light sparking within.

I'm no spring chicken, and I'm still trying to figure out what to do with my life. The difference is, I'm finally listening to my Self, my inner voice and instincts. I still talk with friends, family and experts to solicit inputs and advice; what's changed is my perception. Rather than erroneously believe my actions are dependent on the advice, I try now to absorb all inputs and consider them in light of what feels right to me.

It makes all the difference in the world.

If you mess up your children, nothing else you do really matters

—Jacqueline Kennedy Onassis

BECOMING A PARENT completely changes your life. We've all heard that. Intuiting the implications, though, requires personal experience. We cannot appreciate how profound the shift to parenthood is without becoming a parent. This is true for all rites of passage and applies to all relationships—personal and professional.

- We don't have to be great parents to have great kids, we just have to be good;
- We don't have to be great managers to have great teams, we just have to be good;
- We don't have to be great planners to have a great life, we just have to be good.

We bring positive energy into our lives and into the world when we are kind and patient.

It is never a mistake to breathe and slow, to have patience with others: children who are over-excited or frightened; elderly parents or neighbors who are forgetful or who need help with daily tasks; those who are psychologically or emotionally scarred or damaged; even pets who are scared of storms or strangers.

"*It is never a mistake to breathe.*"

By listening and working to understand what others are going through, we avoid the buildup of tensions and frustrations that push us to lash out with anger or hostility. Being a good parent, a good child, a good friend, a good passerby suggests a challenge as we rush along in a headlong race to 'accomplish' and to 'succeed,' but what does 'succeed' mean?

Personally, I think success is making a positive difference in someone's life. By that measure, taking time is an accomplishment in and of itself.

Most important: no job is ever more important than the people we love.

Put on your oxygen mask first
—Every airline

IT'S HARD TO figure out the right balance of self-care vs. putting others first. When the slings and arrows of daily existence overwhelm us, that is the moment we must gift ourselves a respite—a hot shower or warm bath, a long walk, an hour curled up with a book. If we don't, we may inadvertently take our frustrations out on others.

> "Patience and unconditional love are a winning combination."

Life is short. Life is hard. Life holds both joy and sorrows. We all experience trials and tribulations. It's how we choose to handle these ups and downs that defines us—not anyone or anything else. Just us.

Giving ourselves the luxury of some 'me time' may seem selfish, however, self-gifting a few minutes returns multifold on the investment by allowing our blood pressure to drop, our breathing to slow, and our brains to clear. We find that instead of yelling at a child or store clerk or complete stranger, we are able to smile and realize the situation is not as grave or significant as we first believed.

Every living being is unique, so what works to calm or center one person may not work for another. The trick is to find what works for us, then allow ourselves to indulge in enough self-care to remain positive throughout our journey to be the best person we can be.

Patience and unconditional love are a winning combination.

You've got to eat a peck of dirt before you die
—Rev. Rhys Price

MY GRANDFATHER, RHYS Price, was a Presbyterian minister from a Welsh coal mining family. He grew up between the two world wars. Everyone in his family, everyone he knew, nearly everyone in the U.K. it seemed, had a Victory Garden. When he and my grandmother emigrated to the U.S., they planted a wonderful garden full of tomatoes, corn, snap peas, potatoes, onions, and more.

The garden was bigger than the living room of their modest home.

In our early years, we grandkids spent our summers in Cape May, NJ, where his Parish was. We spent hours picking ripened veggies from the ground, brushing off the dirt, and inevitably eating half of what we picked. We played in the rain, explored the nearby woods, and invented all sorts of games to play. Having that kind of freedom seems to be less and less possible in the world today. Too many people and too much social media (all those 'fabulous' people being fabulous all the time ... seriously?).

We, kids and adults alike, have become disconnected, have too little unstructured play and relaxation time, spend too little time having fun.

When my husband and I looked for pre-schools for our kids, most schools touted their rigorous academic regimes. Surely making a two-year-old literally color within the lines does little to foster creativity; structuring days with nearly every minute filled with 'educational' activities does nothing to boost imaginative thought; having a playground comprised of a black top surrounded by a fence where each child is given a ball does little to foster independent thinking.

We wanted our children to learn and grow so they could be happy and well-adjusted.

In the end, we opted not to send our kids to these 'top preschools.' Instead, we chose to send them to the preschools with the best and biggest playgrounds; ones that were messy and colorful, that allowed for lots of unstructured playtime, and where the teachers were kind and not disciplinarians.

Today, as my children journey along their own life paths, they become increasingly compassionate and caring, creative and inquisitive.

I couldn't be prouder.

The young do not know enough to be prudent; and, therefore, they attempt the impossible—and achieve it, generation after generation

—Pearl S. Buck

HAVING FUN, WE'VE been told, means we're not being productive and will never succeed. But is that true? What does it really mean to be productive? On a farm, it's the output of crops or livestock; in business, it's producing goods or services; in economics, it has to do with capital appreciation. How about in life?

> "If we are to be successful, we must be happy."

What does it mean to live a productive and successful life?

Our society vastly overvalues wealth and material goods, often at the expense of family and leisure time.

To me, being truly successful means being happy, feeling deeply satisfied with what I'm doing and who I'm doing it with.

Not only that, I believe wholeheartedly that having fun by engaging in recreational activities is critical to living 'productively.' To recreate means to re-create, to re-make and re-new ourselves. If we are to be successful, we must be happy and feel fulfilled; we must take time for play, for self-reflection, for sport, for family, and for ourselves.

> *"Life is short. Have fun...*
> *take a chance and make a changes."*

Coloring outside the lines, having unstructured time to think and play, and surrounding ourselves with positive people frees our minds to think great thoughts. It allows us to recognize inner yearnings, identify our dreams, and gain insights into our path towards self-fulfillment—towards achieving whatever our aspirations are.

Life is short. Have fun. The first part of taking charge of our lives is the worst part: change, which is hard. It's hard because we are stepping into the unknown, yet there's no point in worrying or stressing about what doesn't yet exist, so take a chance and make a change.

I like nonsense. It wakes up the brain cells

—Dr. Seuss

HERE'S A FUN fact: the number of neurons in our brains is equivalent to the number of stars in the galaxy. What an amazing capacity we have to be creative and imaginative! Yet, how many of us take advantage of our unique capabilities for being and doing?

"Each of us has a gift."

Freeing our minds doesn't mean not doing the shopping, cooking, laundry, pick-up/drop off, paying bills, etc. What it does mean is that by taking time to let our minds wander, we can avoid total immersion in our daily grinds, liberating our subconscious to perceive what 'success' means to us.

By allowing ourselves a bit of free time, our subconsciousness may unveil a deep desire or talent we hadn't previously acknowledged or understood. Opening ourselves and our minds can release infinite insights into who we are and what we truly want to do and be.

Each of us has a gift and, even though each of our gifts differ, everyone has the potential to excel in some way and love doing it.

> *"Whatever your dream is,*
> *be bold!"*

Once we know our ambition, we can take that first step: deciding to make a change. As long as we continue to make choices that are right for us, consistently and over the long term, we are moving in the right direction.

Whatever your dream is, be bold! Take charge of your destiny and don't let naysayers or circumstance drag you down or pull you away.

Safe Home Now

—Nancy (Ann) Aitcheson Price

MY GRANDMOTHER, NANCY Price, was born in Edinburgh in 1908. She was an active and outgoing young woman who served as a Red Cross nurse during WW2. She emigrated to the U.S. with my grandfather in the 1950s. In 1965, they moved to Cape May, NJ, where they stayed until my grandfather died. The family congregated at their home for holidays and vacations.

One Thanksgiving, my grandmother looked sharply at my cousins, sister, and me and said: "all joints on the table will be carved!"

We kids had heard this many times; since we had no clue what it meant, our response was a collective blank stare. On this occasion, however, she pursed her lips, sighed, and said: "take your elbows off the table." We did. She gave a small nod, smiled and said: "It's about time! I'd hate to have had to carve them off, though I guess arms would be less heavy than legs" (chuckle, chuckle). Uhm …

"Nancy!" my grandfather admonished, "can we not have stories about cut off legs at the dinner table?"

"Remarkably heavy" she said winking at us and chuckling again.

When she was a wartime nurse, she assisted in surgeries. The first time a doctor handed her a dismembered leg, it turned out to be heavier than she'd anticipated, and she ended up falling backwards and landing flat on her backside on the floor. The event wasn't funny in the moment, yet when she finally told me the story years and years later, she was laughing. Cop humor ... gallows humor ... finding a way to deal with horrors without losing one's mind.

I share this story because, in spite of being raised by the generation that suffered the atrocities of WW1, and living through active bombing in London in WW2; in spite of following her husband across 'the Pond' and having to start over several times as they moved around the country; in spite of losing her husband in 1978, and having to learn how to live on her own; and, in spite of all the highs and lows we all face on a daily basis, my grandmother lived a happy, long, and healthy life.

Until her early 90s, grandmother walked a mile a day, was active in her church group, socialized, actively engaged in her children's and grandchildren's lives, wrote at least one letter to a distant friend or relative every day, completed a daily crossword and word-find puzzle, and waited until the 6pm news to turn on the television, which she always turned off after Jeopardy.

I try to emulate her personal fortitude, her commitment and drive. As I sit at the computer typing these words, munching on chips and listening to the indistinct murmur of voices on the television playing in the background, my efforts pale, but effort counts. Attitude counts. Positivity counts. Self-love and self-acceptance count.

The bottom line is that we don't have to be fabulous to have fabulous outcomes.

A final word

THANK YOU FOR taking the time to read my book!

I wrote this book with the intent of empowering readers to embrace choosing to see the half-full glass, to know there is gladness among the misery, and to understand we have the power to be genuinely happy and fulfilled.

Why?

Because we are the only ones who can define what happiness is for us, and because achieving goals that bring us joy is the absolute definition of personal success.

If even one kernel of wisdom helped you in any small way, then I have succeeded. If not, well… that's okay. I've done my best.

> *"We are the only ones who can define what happiness is for us."*

If you have a few minutes, please consider leaving an honest online review. It can be brief—as little as a sentence or two. By sharing if you liked this book or not and why, you help other readers decide if *It's Okay Not to Be Fabulous Every Day!* is right for them.

I read all comments, so look forward to hearing from you.

Thank you again, Ally.

Acknowledgements

First and foremost, I want to thank my amazing children, Kyle and Isabel, for their love, their hugs, their emotional support, and their validation of my worth as a parent and a person. Thank you for all the typo and content checks, and for encouraging me to put these words into book form so it could be shared with others.

Thanks also to Bethany and especially Steve at Telemachus Press for their incredible patience with me as I crawled up the learning curve ladder on my way to becoming a first-time published author.

To my friends who read early versions, thank you for your comments and encouragement—your input helped make this a better read.

And, finally, I want to thank my mother. She and I spoke every day for decades and, for the final months of her life, she lived with me. It is an incredible irony—one she would have appreciated—that not being able to pour my heart out to her was a significant impetus for pouring my words onto paper.

About the Author

Ally Dalsimer is a former award-winning environmental professional and Candidate for Congress. Currently, Ally is a motivational coach who empowers others to overcome their barriers and find fulfillment in their lives. *It's Okay Not to Be Fabulous Every Day!* is Ally's first book. Learn more at AllyDalsimer.com and at Ally.Dalsimer on Instagram.

About the Artist

Lea Waldridge is an artist and educator. She studied at the Minneapolis College of Arts and Design, and currently lives in the DC metro area. See more at Lea_Waldridge on Instagram.

Ingram Content Group UK Ltd.
Milton Keynes UK
UKHW010610020523
421079UK00003B/109